GEORGE FRIDERIC HANDEL

THE WATER MUSIC

SOLO PIANO

Arranged by
ARTHUR CAMPBELL

EDITION PETERS

LONDON

Frankfurt   New York

CONTENTS

The Water Music

I: Air

G. F. Handel
arr. Arthur Campbell

Edition Peters No. 7345

II: Adagio

III: Menuet

2nd time

1.

2.

2nd time

1.

2.

Fine

Da capo al fine

6

IV: Bourrée

V: Andante

VI: Menuet

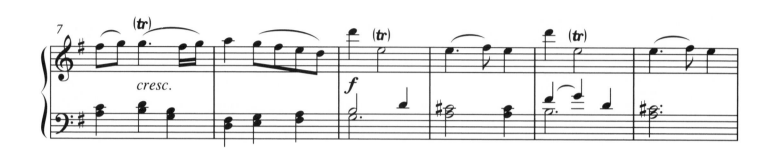

Fine

Da capo al fine

VII: Hornpipe

VIII: Gigue

Da capo al fine

IX: Menuet

Da capo al fine

X: Alla Hornpipe

14

Halstan & Co. Ltd., Amersham, Bucks., England